Music

KINGFISHER

First published 2011 by Kingfisher
an imprint of Macmillan Children's Books
a division of Macmillan Publishers Limited
20 New Wharf Road, London N1 9RR
Basingstoke and Oxford
Associated companies throughout the world
www.panmacmillan.com

ISBN 978-0-7534-3083-5

Consultant: Kwêsi Edman

Designed and created by Basher www.basherbooks.com
Text written by Dan Green

Dedicated to my Dad

Text and design copyright © Toucan Books Ltd 2011
Based on an original concept by Toucan Books Ltd
Illustrations copyright © Simon Basher 2011

9 8 7 6 5 4 3 2 1
1TR/0411/UG/WKT/140MA

A CIP catalogue record for this book
is available from the British Library.

Printed in China

Note to readers: the website addresses listed above are correct at
the time of going to print. However, due to the ever-changing nature
of the internet, website addresses and content can change. Websites
can contain links that are unsuitable for children. The publisher cannot
be held responsible for changes in website addresses or content, or for
information obtained through a third party. We strongly advise that
internet searches should be supervised by an adult.

CONTENTS

Introduction

Music

Everyone loves a good tune, but just what is music? It's tricky to put into words, that's for sure. Every so often, out of the blue, a song flashes into your head. But, just like a slippery fish spotted beneath the water's surface, the moment you try to grab it – to make sense of how it got there – it's gone. That's because music often relates to how you are feeling. A song might pop up when you're happy or sad, over the moon or uneasy about something. Or it could just be the last song you heard on the radio before leaving the house for school!

Wolfgang Amadeus Mozart (1756–91) understood that music is in each and every one of us. But he also knew that to express it and get those feelings *just* right would take a lifetime of study and practice. And boy, did he start early! He composed his first piece of music at the age of five, and by the time he died, aged 35, he had penned more than 600 concertos, operas, ballets and symphonies. Phew! It wasn't all old-fashioned dance music for people in silly tights and wigs either – many are masterpieces loved by millions. Come on, it's time to face the music!

Mozart

Sound

* Cacophonous character created by vibrating air molecules
* Has four traits: pitch, volume, timbre, sound-source location
* You are surrounded by this guy wherever you go

I'm the "vibey" kinda dude that really gets a place buzzin'. Your world is alive with my hullabaloo: sirens; mobile phones; the hum of traffic and squeal of brakes; the rhubarb-rhubarb of people chattering; cups, plates and cutlery clattering. Out in the countryside, there I am again, in birdsong, flowing rivers, rain and thunder.

At my most basic, I am a vibration – a disturbance in molecules of air that travels to your ear. You can make me by hitting a drum, blowing through a tube, plucking a string or just by clapping your hands – anything that generates energy to move molecules in the air. Music takes me one magical step further. It goes beyond making sound to create textures and combinations that speak to the emotions. Just feel those vibes!

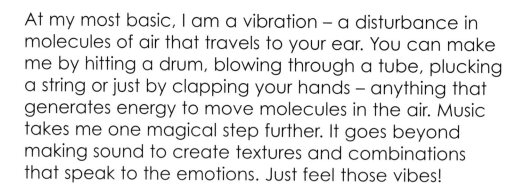

● Speed of sound in air: 330 m/s
● Deepest concert ever: 303 m below sea level (Katie Melua, 2006)
● World's largest and loudest instrument: Atlantic City Boardwalk Hall Organ

Sound

Chapter 1
■ Musical Marvels

Sound is nothing more than disturbances and pulses travelling through the air, but thanks to this bunch of movers and shakers, it can be high or low, short or long, jerky or smooth. These Musical Marvels are Sound's essential building blocks – let it be said – the very *sounds* of music! Blasts of Sound of different length give you all-important Rhythm. Add Tempo, Pitch and Dynamics and things really start to hum. Throw in a catchy Melody and some pure, sweet Harmony, and lace the whole lot with a little magic ingredient – silence. It'll be music to your ears. But let's hear the Marvels speak for themselves.

Pitch

Tempo

Rhythm

Dynamics

Melody

Harmony

Pitch

Musical Marvels

✷ The most basic quality of a sound – how high or low it is
✷ A single sound at an unchanging pitch is called a note
✷ Pitch is measured in Hertz (Hz) but notes known by letters A–G

I am the first thing you notice about Sound – how high or low it is. But, beware, for in the wrong hands, I can be a dangerous weapon!

I'm what makes Note sound clear and regular, and I'm all about good vibrations. The more vibrations per second, the higher the sound of the note you hear. Twang a short string or blow a short pipe, and Note goes high. A wide, thick or long string or pipe has the opposite effect, with Note heading way down low. While musical sound is *pitched* just at the right level, some sounds are above the range of hearing (ultrasonic) and others are beneath it (infrasonic). Very high sounds can be painfully piercing and very low sounds might make you short of breath, want to be sick or even lose your balance.

● Concert pitch: 440 Hz (A above middle C)
● Range of human hearing: 25–20,000 Hz
● Scientific name for pitch: frequency

Pitch

Tempo
Musical Marvels

- ✹ This musical pacemaker sets the speed of a tune
- ✹ Measured in beats per minute (bpm)
- ✹ Instructions for tempo are written above a piece of music

What-o! I love a thumping good beat. With a stiff upper lip and military precision, I march to the sound of the drum. I set the pace of a tune and make sure that everyone sticks to it.

Most music keeps to a regular beat – a "click" that you can tap with your feet or snap with your fingers. Swingin' Rhythm uses my rat-tat-tat as a foundation for music's elaborate grooves. Without my steady beat to sustain them, his creative patterns would falter and flounder. I'm a technical whiz, too: the faster I go, the more difficult a piece of music is to play. It's down to me to hold it all together. With me in charge, no one gets ahead of the beat (rushing) or falls behind (dragging), so get in line now. Hup, two, three, four, hup...

- ● Average heart rate: 60–80 bpm
- ● *Andante* (walking pace): 80–104 bpm
- ● Well-known tempi: *adagio* (slow), *vivace* (lively), *presto* (fast)

Tempo

Rhythm

Musical Marvels

- ✳ Jumpy fella who gets the party going with a swing
- ✳ The dude that keeps music moving along
- ✳ Made of notes and silences of different duration

Right on the beat, it's me who gets you outta your seat, wigglin' your hips and tappin' your feet. The king of swing, I'm all about movement and sway.

You see, all music has a step to it, a kinda lilt that keeps it movin' along. And this is the magic I sprinkle. Simple or complex, I use combinations of sound and silence to make patterns that get repeated over and over, or can change at a whim. I'm nothing like that robot, Tempo, who just ticks time, no sir! Played with real feeeelin', I get right into the groove using tension and release. It's me that keeps the words of a song flowing in time with the music. Listen to your heart beat its steady lub-dub, lub-dub and you'll find ME – a rhythm of your very own! Every natural movement has these throbs and accents. Lubba dubba!

- ● Metre: the division of music into equal beats when written down
- ● Bar (measure): a section of music with a given number of beats
- ● Time signature: indicates the number and type of beats in a bar

Rhythm

Dynamics
■ Musical Marvels

☀ This musical dynamo controls the volume of sounds
☀ Bold and brash at times, can also be stirring and emotional
☀ *Crescendo* (<) increases volume; *diminuendo* (>) decreases it

HI THERE *ff*ANS! I'm *ff*lamboyant and expressive, and I love to make a noise – loud or soft. You see, I have my *ff*inger on the volume knob. I can swell to capacity, lifting the chest and putting a sparkle in the eye. Or I can diminish to a whisper for a more intimate feel.

I control the decibels (dB) – that's the volume setting to you. My instructions are written in Italian above the stave for musicians to follow: *forte* (*f*) for playing loud and proud; *piano* (*p*) for playing nice and soft. Thunderous *fortissimo* (*ff*) (VERY LOUD) sounds are my *ff*avourite, as you can probably tell! But, please, take care: at EXTREMELY LOUD volumes I can make your eyeballs vibrate in their sockets. If you're not careful, I can mess with your vision and harm your ears. A little *too* dynamic, perhaps?

● Soft whisper: 30 dB
● Front row at a rock concert: 110 dB
● Volume that can instantly pierce your eardrum: 160 dB

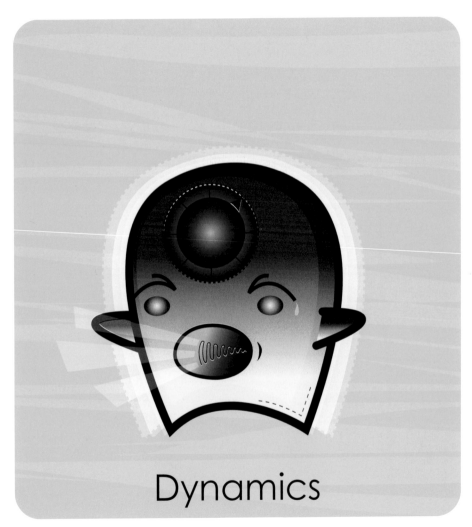

Dynamics

Melody
■ Musical Marvels

✳ This chirpy chappie holds the secret of a good tune
✳ A short, catchy, musical phrase that gets repeated in a song
✳ Can be used as a theme, arranged in different variations

Catchy and irresistible, I'm all hook! Always at the heart of a tune, I'm the bit of music that you can hum.

I tend to stick in your head; you just can't help hearing me long after I've been played. My sweet sounds speak to something deep inside your brain and I lodge right in there, popping up when you least expect it. I use sequences of notes at different pitches to construct little ditties. My simplest versions are single lines, like the nursery rhymes you used to sing. You'll find all of the Musical Marvels embedded in my phrasing – that is, the pattern of my notes. Different styles of music use me in different ways, mixing me with Rhythm and Harmony. Catchy and irresistible, I'm all hook. Sorry? Did I say that already? Well, I do have a habit of repeating myself!

● Monophonic music: a single melody played on its own
● Polyphonic music: two or more melodies played at the same time
● Homophonic music: a melody played with harmony added

Melody

Harmony
Musical Marvels

* Name derives from Greek *harmonia*, meaning agreement
* Supports the melody of a tune
* The biggest influence on the mood of a piece of music

Melody and I are the best of friends. She tends to hog the limelight, sure, but we get along so well that I'm always happy to play second fiddle!

I can be very subtle and am often overlooked – you don't always realize I'm there – but I do a lot to colour the sounds you hear. It's because of me that music makes you feel a certain way. I can infuse a tune with sad, sombre inflections or bolster a ditty with bright, brassy washes. My trick is to layer Pitch on top of Melody's tinkling line of notes. My careful choice of when to match or partner one note with another determines whether Melody's line has a smooth jazzy feel to it or has the moody blues! From the pride-of-the-nation to spooked-out scary, you can certainly rely on me to stir up the emotions!

- Harmonies made up of two musical threads include Bach's two-part inventions
- Discordant harmony: used in much 20th- and 21st-century music
- Chorus: made up of several harmonious sounds of a similar pitch

Harmony

Chapter 2
■ Noteworthy Nerds

Notorious, notable and nifty, the Noteworthy Nerds are a bunch of well-meaning geeks. They spend their time on a grid of lines and gaps called a stave. Using a treble clef for the high notes and a bass clef for the low ones, the stave carries all the information needed to play a piece of music. It's a confusion of lines, dots and dashes to start with, but you'll soon crack this crew. Learning to read music is just like scanning and understanding text on a page. A practised musician reads a sheet of music like a story, just like you're reading this now. Don't be scared, come and meet the Nerds. They don't bite… often!

Note

Rest

Scale

Sharp

Flat

Interval

Chord

Time Signature

Note

■ Noteworthy Nerds

✳ A single, pure and unwavering pitch
✳ Has both pitch (high or low) and duration (long or short)
✳ Almost all music is made using just 12 different notes

I am one "note-able" personage, believe me! The most basic building block of all music – nothing gets made or played without me.

Always dressed in black, I sit on, and between, the lines of a musical stave. My rounded forms can be solid or hollow, and I often come with a fancy-looking tail or have a dot by my side. I am the perfect combination of Pitch and duration. My most familiar form is a crotchet. Four of these little critters make a semibreve. Two crotchets make a minim and half a crotchet is a quaver. I also have different names, determined by Pitch. Seven natural notes make up Scale and are called A, B, C, D, E, F and G, while my pals, Sharp and Flat, make up the half-tones in between.

● Flag: a tail attached to a stem, denoting duration
● Dot: follows a note to indicate that it is one-and-a-half times the value shown
● CABBAGED: the longest word that can be played on a musical instrument

Note

Rest
■ Noteworthy Nerds

☀ This laid-back fella lounges about on the musical stave
☀ Signals a silence in the music
☀ Tells musicians how long to pause

Hush now! I am the silent partner in this business of music-making. You can spot me leaning lazily against the lines of the stave. When musicians see me, they know it's time for a breather and they pause for a break.

Call me an idler if you like, but I'm no lazybones! Silence is golden and all that, but it also happens to be half of what makes Rhythm jump. The bits of music where nobody plays work just as hard as when the musicians saw and puff and bang away. Every bit as clever as Note, I come in different values, or sizes, to tell players how long they need to pause. Like Note, I am organized into semibreves, minims, crotchets, quavers and so forth. A dot next to me shows that I'm one-and-a-half times the value shown. The "rest" is up to you!

● Semibreve rest: a rest with the value of four crotchets
● Breve rest: a rest with the value of eight crotchets
● Lunga rest: a rest with the value of sixteen crotchets

Rest

Scale

■ Noteworthy Nerds

✴ A scale is a doh-ray-mi sequence of notes
✴ Major scales use a different note pattern to minor scales
✴ All notes in any scale make up its key signature

I'm mad as a yo-yo, galloping up and down the musical stave playing specific patterns of notes. If you learn a musical instrument, you'll practise me over and over.

My entire being relies on one solid, scientific fact: take any note, double its frequency and it has the same (but higher pitched) sound as the first. Two such notes top and tail an octave, which is made up of eight whole tones with five semitones in between. Together the twelve notes are just like a flight of stairs, where top and bottom steps have the same sound. Usually, I bound up and down using only seven steps (the eighth is always the octave, or top step), but I can use patterns of just five or even all twelve. The steps I choose form my character – major patterns sound bright and happy, while minor keys have a melancholy air.

● Number of notes in a typical scale: 7
● Number of notes in a chromatic scale: 12
● Number of notes in a pentatonic scale: 5

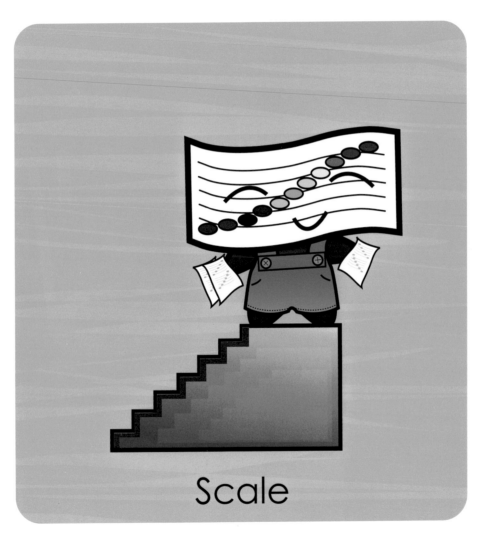

Scale

Sharp

■ Noteworthy Nerds

✳ Keen-bean twin who is a note raised by a half-tone
✳ Can be found on the black keys of a piano (as can Flat)
✳ When singing, sharp notes overshoot the correct note

Don't make a *hash* of it – I'm no boring #! You hear me when I occur as a passing accidental, but there's nothing random about me. My snazzy notes pop out of the key signature deliberately. I'm a cut above Flat, my half-tone brother. While he stands downwind of a natural note of the same name, I am pitched a half-tone higher. That's me, looking sharp!

Sharp

● Written as ♯ and placed to the left of the note to be played
● Not marked by each note if it already appears in the key signature
● Double sharp: raises the note by two half-tones

Flat

Noteworthy Nerds

- ❋ The cooler brother of the black-key twins
- ❋ A note that has been lowered by a half-tone
- ❋ When singing, a flat note does not reach the correct note

Flat

I am one hep cat and hang out on the black keys of a piano, among other places. While Sharp overshoots the natural note, I never quite reach it. Instead I end up a half-tone lower. I'm accidental – that is, on purpose, but out of key – and sound cool in the right places. Take care, though: if you hit a flat when it should be a natural, musicians call me a bum note!

- ● Written as ♭ and positioned just the same as for a sharp
- ● Double flat: lowers the note by two half-tones
- ● A soft-sounding note in contrast to a sharp's brighter sound

Interval

✳ The difference in pitch between two musical sounds
✳ Played one after the other, or together, to build harmonies
✳ Closely related to scales

I'm the space between each of stair-bounding Scale's steps. I indicate the difference in pitch from one note to the next. You can work me out by counting the stave lines and spaces between the two notes. My name depends on however many there are – thirds, fourths, fifths – but you have to remember to count the one each note is on, too! Mind that gap!

Interval

● Smallest interval: half-step or semitone
● Harmonic interval: when the two notes are played at the same time
● Melodic interval: when one of the notes is played after the other

Chord

Noteworthy Nerds ■

* A team of three or more notes, all played at the same time
* Has a major or minor feel, depending on the intervals used
* Plays a starring role in most rock music

Chord

So much for plain Jane Interval, with her two-tone Harmony! You'll be flippin' your lid for my combos of three or more! I layer up Sound to thrill your ears. Here's my secret: I take a single note (called the root) and add Interval to create Harmony. Then I add another note, plus Interval, and so on, until I have a jolly stack of these mini musical clusters! Bet that strikes the right chord!

● *Arpeggio*: notes of a chord played separately
● Most common chords: major and minor triads – that is, chords of three notes
● Discord: when notes that are not harmonious are played at the same time

Time Signature
■ Noteworthy Nerds

✴ There's no beating this strict counting band master
✴ Sets the beat, the bar and note value of the beat
✴ Combines with rhythm to create different musical styles

I'm one serious vibester, a time-counting hipster who really likes to get on down. I divide music into repeating sets of beats, called bars. Musicians use me to keep in time with each other.

This is how I operate: I sit at the front of a musical stave, just after the clef sign. I'm made of two numbers – one on top of the other. My top number tells you how many beats to count before repeating. My bottom number lets you know the value of each of those beats – that is, whether it lasts a minim, a crotchet, a quaver and so on. Three crotchets to a bar (3/4 time signature) creates a waltz beat. But I can also polka (2/4), rock (4/4), jig (6/8) and more – you'll soon be able to tell my musical flavour at a glance. It's all a matter of time!

● 4/4: also called common time
● *Mission Impossible* theme: 5/4
● Stravinsky's 1913 *The Rite of Spring* caused a riot because of its time changes!

Time Signature

Chapter 3
■ Rowdy Bunch

Put your hands together for this jinglin', jammin' crew,
the guys who just love to be picked up and played.
In this Rowdy Bunch you'll find all the different classes
of music-making instrument, each with its own funky
and interesting way of getting air to vibrate to create
Sound. Let's hear it for the silky Strings, gentle Woodwind
and the bold-as Brass. And, please, let's not forget
crashing, bashing Percussion and that old sweetie,
Piano. You've got your own dear Voice, too, of course.
There's nothing like playing together in a group to
create fine sounds. Hey, that's them tuning up now!

Voice

Piano

Strings

Woodwind

Brass

Percussion

Voice

■ Rowdy Bunch

☀ Your in-built musical instrument
☀ You mix voice and music with words to get all-powerful song
☀ Produced using a combination of vocal cords and cavities

I am your in-built boom-box – the most basic of all musical instruments and the world's only fully natural one. And boy, am I powerful; with me in full voice, things can get loud, raw and raucous, believe me!

Put me to music, and I really start to sing! Soprano is my high register; alto brings rich harmonies; tenors become famous (male) opera singers; and basses are the guys with voices deep in their boots. *Anyone* can use me. You have two tiny elastic strips of cartilage in your throat – your vocal cords. They only make a small squeak, but the caverns of your mouth, nose and throat amplify the sound to a howl. I'm fully automatic – just imagining the sound you want to make is enough to tense your vocal cords to exactly the right pitch. You should be singing my praises!

● Soprano frequency: 2500 Hz and above
● Length of each vocal cord: 1.25 cm
● Number of muscles in the throat and mouth: 60

Voice

Piano

Rowdy Bunch

✴ The world's most popular musical instrument
✴ Solo and accompaniment instrument in one package
✴ Can be played by one or two people in a duet

They say an opera's never over 'til the fat lady sings and it is a sentiment I share, for I am the grand old dame of this Rowdy Bunch. You can call me Joanna!

I'm a smooth and sassy sophisticate. Tickle my ebonies and ivories and you'll see why. As a grand piano I take pride of place, sitting serenely on a concert stage, all polished black curves and shimmering surfaces. But I feel equally at home in my upright form at school or in a busy bluesy bar. I make sounds using wires, but I'm no ordinary stringed instrument. Look under my hood, and you'll find that I'm in a class of my own. For every note played, I have a felt-covered hammer that strikes one, two or three strings at a time. And I have pedals that can dampen my sound or let my notes ring out. My song is sung!

● Invented by: Bartolomeo Cristofori (1709)
● Number of keys: 88 (52 white and 36 black)
● Length of a grand piano: 2.2–3 m

Piano

Strings
■ Rowdy Bunch

✳ Family of musical instruments with stretched lengths of string
✳ Plucked or bowed, this lot are (mostly) light and portable
✳ The proper name for a stringed instrument is a chordophone

We're all of a quiver! Built around lengths of twanging gut, we're one big, happy, musical family. Here you've got your guitars (including mandolins, banjos, ukeleles and lutes). And there you've got your violins (with violas, cellos and double basses). In the middle is old lady harp (she's the one that's not so portable).

We're a scratchy lot, and it's hard for us to stop fidgeting and fiddling! We make our sound using different lengths and thicknesses of taut strings and cords. The shorter, thinner and tighter the string, the higher the pitch of the note produced. Making a wire vibrate by plucking or hitting it is an obvious ploy (Piano has learnt a thing or two from us). Far more stylish is using a bow laced with sticky rosin. Difficult to play? Fiddlesticks!

● Number of stringed instruments in full orchestra: up to 60
● Most strings on one instrument: 48 (harp)
● Fewest strings: 1 (ektara or mouth bow)

Strings

Woodwind
■ Rowdy Bunch

* ✳ Instruments that make sound using a tube with holes in it
* ✳ Their music appears at the top of a full orchestral score
* ✳ Proper name for a woodwind instrument is an aerophone

We're a bunch of reedy warblers, airy and filled to the brim with trills and swells. Life's a breeze for us! We've got the tin whistle, recorder, flute, clarinet, oboe, saxophone, bassoon and bagpipes. Some of us are made of metal and not wood, despite our name. "Wood" you believe it?

We make sound when air vibrates inside a thin tube. Covering over holes in a certain pattern makes our sounds change and lets us hit the right notes. Some of us have lots of metal keys that cover or open the holes. We all produce mellow, velvety smooth tones. Reed instruments (clarinets, oboes, bassoons and saxophones) use a mouthpiece with thin pieces of cane to make the air vibrate, while flutes, recorders and whistles are played by blowing across the top of the tube. Blows your mind!

* ● Oldest wind instrument: didgeridoo
* ● Biggest wind instrument: contrabassoon (5 m of tubing)
* ● Strangest woodwind instrument: Indian nose flute (played with the nose!)

Woodwind

Brass

■ Rowdy Bunch

☀ Brassed-off bunch at the heart of the big band sound
☀ Their music appears in the middle of a full orchestral score
☀ These shiny wind instruments are called aerophones

Big and bold, we're full of bluster. We've got tootin' trumpets, elegant French horns, crooning cornets, and comical trombones, euphoniums and tubas. Each is played by blowing into a mouthpiece. Valves change the length of the tube down which the air travels – the smaller and shorter the pipe, the higher the sound. Big brass band, reggae, soul or jazz: we dig it all. Oom pah pah!

Brass

● Alternative name for brass instruments: labrosones (lip-vibrators)
● Newest brass instrument: vuvuzela
● A tuba's lowest note: 16 Hz – 4 octaves lower than middle C, written as C_0

Percussion

Rowdy Bunch

- ✱ This noisy tribe beats a tattoo to provide rhythm
- ✱ Hit with the hand, beaten with a stick or shaken
- ✱ Also known as membranophones and idiophones

Percussion

We're a tub-thumpin' crew and we're here to make a hullabaloo! Our rhythmic beats form the back line of any band. And our tribe is massive. Besides drums, with skins stretched over tubs, are crashing cymbals and gongs, funky shakers and maracas, whip-crackin' woodblock, chiming glockenspiel, jazzy xylophone and ding-dong bells. Gimme some skin, brother!

- ● Membranophone: any kind of drum with a vibrating skin
- ● Idiophone: an instrument whose entire frame vibrates when struck (e.g. bell)
- ● Strangest percussion instrument: aquaggaswack (29 hanging pot lids)

Chapter 4
■ Sweet Sounds

For many centuries, music has had us toe-tapping, boogaloo-ing and humming along to its ever-changing rhythm. The Sweet Sounds gang is a bulging bag busting with all sorts of different styles, or genres, of music. Some of them are quite similar; some borrow from one another or cross over; and some are a million miles apart. While Classical and Folk are centuries old, other music styles, like Electronic, were born yesterday. Between them they range from strict and formal to freeform – even made up on the spot. They don't all float everybody's boat, but the more you know 'em, the more you'll love 'em!

Classical

Folk

Blues

Jazz

Pop

Electronic
Sounds

Classical
■Sweet Sounds

✴ Flamboyant fellow whose music is formally written down
✴ Examples include concertos, symphonies, sonatas and opera
✴ The composer is all-important in this musical style

I'm cultured, clever and rather wonderful. With my huge variety of different styles, I'm an ace for adverts and mood music in movies. And yet, despite (or perhaps because of) my sophistication, people think I'm a snob.

Well, I must say, I take a certain open-mindedness to be appreciated. For starters, I'm mostly played with musical instruments that were invented before the 19th century. And because I'm always written on paper, I'm stricter than other types of music. This means musicians have to learn how to read and interpret instructions to know how I should be played. Unlike other members of the Sweet Sounds crew, I have little time for improvising (inventing your own bits). Say I'm snooty if you like, but there's no denying that I put the "class"-ical into music!

● First time the word "classical" was used: early 19th century
● Most Grammy Awards won by a classical musician: 31 (conductor Sir Georg Solti)
● Shortest opera: 7 mins 27 secs (Darius Milhaud's *The Deliverance of Theseus*)

Classical

Folk
■ Sweet Sounds

☀ Country music that is passed down by word of mouth
☀ Often celebrates a moment in life – a birth or marriage, say
☀ Most world music can be described as folk

World over, I am the sound of the people, the real voice of music. Wherever you go in the world, you'll find a different version of me that has been passed down from one generation to the next for centuries.

I'm incredibly versatile, so let's ditch that image of checked-shirt-wearing beardies strumming guitars, pickin' banjoes and sawin' away at fiddles! American bluegrass, Moroccan gnoua, klezmer from Eastern Europe, jaunty Venezuelan joropo – no matter how wild the rhythms or how strange the melodies, these gritty, down-to-earth sounds all stem from me. I travel by word of mouth, yet the style and feel of my music always remains the same. Unlike Classical, I don't need to write it down – my music is instinctive, it's all in the genes!

● Meaning of folk: ordinary people
● Ballad: a poem that is sung to a folk tune
● Popular folk instruments include the harmonica, fiddle (violin) and penny whistle

Folk

Blues

■ Sweet Sounds

✳ Musical style that started out as sad slave songs
✳ Originally call-and-response songs sung in the fields
✳ The older cousin of rock music

There's nothing jaunty about me. My sad songs tell of the hardship and suffering of Africans taken to work as slaves in the American South. My blue note is an interval called the minor third. But, hey – sad, yes, tragic, no! My cool echoes are heard in my upbeat brother, Jazz, in gospel music and in rock 'n' roll! From blues to schmooze and doo-wop-diddy-doos.

Blues

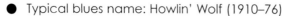

● Typical blues name: Howlin' Wolf (1910–76)
● Influential album: *King of the Delta Blues Singers* (Robert Johnson, 1961)
● The 'Mother' of the Blues was singer Ma Rainey (1886–1939)

Jazz

Sweet Sounds ■

* ✴ This happy American bigshot likes to let the good times roll
* ✴ Loves unusual harmonies and complex rhythms
* ✴ Jazz musicians improvise depending on their mood

Jazz

I'm one smooooooth cat, baby. I get my kicks from hot licks that get a crowd a-jumpin' and a-jivin'. I've been around since the start of the 20th century. Taking my lead from my bro's bluesy sounds, I burst into hundreds of new musical styles with funky names: ragtime, swing, Dixieland, bebop, acid jazz, free jazz and nu-jazz! They all groove to my wildcat beat!

● Birthplace: New Orleans, USA, 1910
● Louis Armstrong's nickname: Satchmo (meaning satchel-mouth)
● First gold record: Chattanooga Choo Choo (Glenn Miller, 1942)

Pop
■ Sweet Sounds

* ☀ This groovy tunester really gets the kids boppin' about
* ☀ Targets the teenage market
* ☀ Usually combines music and voice in a 3–5 minute song

Hey baby, check me out! I'm the brash, glitzy glamour-puss of the Sweet Sounds posse! Out of all our members, I get the most exposure. You can hear me blasting out of radios and on music TV. There's simply no escaping me! I make the tunes you sing in the shower and dance to in front of the mirror.

Ever-popular, I hit the scene in the 1950s as jive-tastic rock 'n' roll. Since that time, I have splintered into a dazzling array of sounds: rock, heavy metal, funk, soul, urban, hip hop, rap, indie, grime, nu-rave, disco, J-Pop, emo, goth, reggae, salsa, reggaeton, punk, merengue, grunge and Motown. There's something for everyone. Chuck in a billion crossover acts and you've got more than enough tribes to drive your parents pop-pop-potty!

● Top-selling single: 37,000,000 (*Candle in the Wind*, Elton John, 1997)
● Most successful songwriting duo: Lennon and McCartney (The Beatles)
● Most Grammy Awards in one year: 8 (Michael Jackson, 1984)

Pop

Electronic Sounds
■ Sweet Sounds

✸ This audio wizard makes sounds using only electronic circuits
✸ Allows you to record music quickly and easily
✸ Electronic instruments use MIDI to talk to one another

I am the future. You'll really flip your switch for my outta-space sounds! I use electronic circuits to generate music, freeing me from the fiddlesome Rowdy Bunch. There's no sound I can't replicate: you just imagine it and my synthesizer circuits do the rest. That's the theory, anyway.

In my youth, my bleeps and tweeks sounded weird, but these days almost every form of music incorporates me somewhere in the mix. Want a pipe organ? Why lug that huge lump around when a small keyboard can do the same trick? I'm best known for dance music – electro, techno, house, rave and trance – but my samplers grab snatches of audio and loop them for hip hop and many other styles. Even rock bands use my sequencers to trigger loops and drumbeats. Just don't pull the plug on me!

● MIDI: Musical Instrument Digital Interface
● Only instrument played without touching: theremin
● Hot-wiring old electronic instruments is called circuit-bending

Electronic Sounds

Index

Character entries are **bold**

Mozart, Wolfgang
  Amadeus 4

N
natural 31, 63
Note 10, 14, 18, **24**, 26, 28,
  30, 31, 32, 33, 40, 42, 44,
  54, 63

O
octave 28, 46, 63

P
Percussion 36, **47**
phrase 18, 63
Piano 30, 31, 36, **40**, 42
Pitch 6, 8, **10**, 18, 20, 24, 30,
  32, 38. 42
Pop **56**

Q
quaver 24, 26, 34

R
Rest **26**
Rhythm 8, 12, **14**, 18, 26, 34,
  47, 48, 52, 55
rock 33, 34, 54, 56, 58
root note 33, 63
rosin 42, 63

S
Scale 24, **28**, 32
score 44, 64
semibreve 24, 26
Sharp 24, **30**, 31
silence 8, 14, 26
song 4, 14, 18, 38, 40, 54,
  56
soprano 64
Sound **6,** 8, 10, 12, 14, 16,
  20, 32, 33, 36, 40, 42, 44,
  46, 52, 55, 56, 58, 64
stave 16, 22, 24, 26, 28, 30,
  32, 34, 64
Strings 36, 40, **42**

T
Tempo 8, **12**, 14,
tenor 64
tension 14, 38, 64
timbre 6, 64
Time Signature 14, **34**,
treble clef 22, 64

V
Voice 36, **38**, 56
volume 6, 16

W
Woodwind 36, **44**

Glossary

Accent When a note or a particular beat in a bar is stressed (played with more weight or force than other notes). An accent is indicated in musical notation using a range of different marks.

Accidental Sharps and flats are also referred to as accidentals. The word describes a note that is raised (sharpened) or lowered (flattened) normally by a semitone. Such notes are out of the key signature.

Alto A singing voice that is the second highest in a piece of music sung in four parts (soprano, alto, tenor, bass). Usually sung by women.

Bars Small sections of musical notation, also known as measures. Each one lasts an equal length of time and contains the same number of beats. A vertical line on the stave indicates the end of a bar.

Bass A singing voice that is the lowest in a piece of music sung in four parts. Usually sung by men.

Bass clef A symbol that indicates the notes are bass (low) notes. On the piano, music with a bass clef is usually played with the left hand.

Beat The rhythmic pulse that lies behind all music. The tempo of a piece of music is described in words or, more accurately, in beats per minute (bpm).

Composer A person who writes music.

Conductor A person who directs an orchestra.

Decibel (dB) Unit that measures the intensity of a sound.

Duet A piece of music intended to be played or sung by two people.

Duration The length of time for which a note, beat or rest lasts.

Frequency The rate at which an instrument or sound wave vibrates; the higher the frequency, the higher the pitch of the resulting sound.

Hertz (Hz) The unit used to measure frequency.

Improvisation Creating music without preparation, or making it up as you go along.

Key The set of notes that together make up a musical scale. The key gives the music a particular feel.

Key signature Always given at the beginning (left-hand side) of the stave, the key signature tells you which set of notes the piece of music uses.

Major key A key signature that creates a happy, upbeat mood.

Measures Another word for bars.

Minor key A key signature that creates a sad or brooding feeling.

Natural A note that is not sharpened or flattened.

Note value Duration for which a note (or rest) is played.

Octave The interval between two notes that sound the same; eight notes make a full octave.

Phrase A short part of a musical tune; a repeating pattern on notes.

Glossary

Root note The particular note around which a scale or chord is based.

Rosin An amber-coloured resin used to coat the bows of stringed instruments.

Score The printed musical notation for a piece of music. It has separate instructions for all the instruments of an orchestra, telling them what and how to play.

Semitone The smallest interval used in Western music. A twelfth of an octave. Also known as a half-tone.

Soprano A singing voice that is the highest in a piece of music sung in four parts. Usually sung by women.

Sound-source location This identifies where a sound is coming from.

Stave Five parallel lines with spaces in between and divided into bars. Notes are written on the lines and in the spaces to indicate their pitch. Also called staff.

Tenor A singing voice that is second lowest in a piece of music sung in four parts. Usually sung by men.

Tension When something is stretched tight.

Timbre The tone or quality of a sound. A trumpet and a guitar sound very different, even when playing the same note and are said to have a different timbre.

Treble clef A symbol that indicates the notes are treble (high) notes. On the piano, music with a treble clef is usually played with the right hand.